Steven Colborne was born in 19  He grew up in Abingdon near O: to study in 2000. He is a grad Westminster, and has undertakei the University of London. Steven's industry, but more recently he has ..ɔı a number of national charities.

He currently lives in South London, not far from Springfield psychiatric hospital where he has been an inpatient on several occasions since his first psychotic episode in 2007. *The Philosophy of a Mad Man* is Steven's first book.

THE
PHILOSOPHY
OF A
MAD MAN

STEVEN COLBORNE

SilverWood

Published in paperback 2012 by SilverWood Books, Bristol, BS1 4HJ
www.silverwoodbooks.co.uk

Many of the names mentioned in this book have been changed in order to
protect people's identities.

ISBN 978-1-78132-023-5

British Library Cataloguing in Publication Data
A CIP catalogue record for this book is available from the British Library

Set in Sabon by SilverWood Books
Printed on paper sourced responsibly

For all who suffer

Contents

Part Two: My Philosophy

Acknowledgements

My heartfelt thanks go out to my good friend Chris Berry and my sister Femke for reading the manuscript and offering feedback and useful suggestions. I am grateful to Jane Wyatt for her kind assistance with proofreading the manuscript. Thanks also to Helen Hart and the team at SilverWood Books for working with me so helpfully and enthusiastically on the publication of this book.

Living with mental health problems can be challenging, but the last few years have been made easier thanks to the support of several good doctors, kind friends (thanks in particular to Helen, Gregg, Claire, and Graham), supportive family (thanks to my father Andrew and his partner Kathryn), and a great psychotherapist (thanks, Tom).

Finally, thanks to you, the reader, for buying this book and dedicating time to reading it. I really appreciate it.

Preface

March 2012

My life so far has been quite a journey. I have experienced the highs and lows of Eastern and Western religious practices and philosophical traditions by immersing myself in the spiritual practices of many different faith groups.

In terms of Eastern faith groups, such practices have included the self-enquiry of Sri Ramana Maharshi, the meditation propounded by the Indian teacher Deepak Chopra, the Zen Buddhist principles of the comparative religion philosopher Alan Watts, the 'shaking meditation' of contemporary Indian teacher Ratu Bagas, and the 'enlightenment' schooling of gurus such as Mooji, Gangaji, and Papaji. In terms of Western traditions, I have been a self-confessed Christian, attending both Protestant and Catholic churches, I have studied Philosophy and Religion at a Jesuit Catholic college in London, I have undertaken psychotherapy with a spiritually inclined body psychotherapist, and have undertaken counselling with a Christian counsellor.

I have experienced the highs of ecstatic and hallucinogenic drugs, of deep stages of meditation, and of the love of true friends, and also the lows of suicidal depression, mental disorder and psychological breakdown. Through a mental health condition that I have (currently diagnosed as Schizoaffective disorder), I have experienced psychosis and altered states of reality on a number of occasions. I have

11

developed a unique but also, I am quite convinced, realistic perspective on the way God works within the created universe. Through my life's journey God has demonstrated to me some important truths about His relationship to the world, and I believe that the next step along that journey is to communicate my experiences and views to others in order to help them reach a more in tune understanding of the way God's world works.

I do not claim to know everything, and I believe that there will always be a mysterious element to human life, as we all struggle with difficult questions about suffering, and death, for instance. But the pursuit of philosophical wisdom is as worthwhile today as it was several thousand years ago in the days of Aristotle and Plato. I do not know what posterity will make of me and my philosophy, but I hope that I will be remembered as someone who is humble, open, and honest, and I hope that you will enjoy reading what I have to say.

When writing about God I sometimes use the pronoun 'He'. This is merely a convention – I don't believe God has a particular gender.

Part One

My Journey

1

Shaking with Ratu

November 2004

On my hands and knees, leaning over a small plastic bucket, I am vomiting violently. The blare of fast-paced music and the wailing and yelping of those shaking their bodies behind me provide the soundtrack to my convulsions. I am desperate that the double dose of liquid tobacco solution that I have just squirted up my nostrils will provide a sufficient dose of 'light energy' to allow me to access a place of mental oblivion, and that finally this agonising mess of furious and desperate thoughts will dissolve into an eruption of tears and give way to the peace of mind I so desperately crave.

Just two days ago in this large, carpeted tent in the Devonshire countryside, I had experienced something incredible. As I stood shaking with perhaps 40 other people, music booming at full blast towards us, a sudden wave of blackness passed through my body/mind in a way that was unlike anything I had ever experienced. As this happened, I found myself letting out a primal scream, before bursting into tears and falling to the floor, and crying my eyes out uninhibitedly for around five minutes. As soon as the crying subsided, I found myself laughing hysterically for a further ten minutes. It all happened quite spontaneously. When the laughing subsided, the room and everyone's faces were brighter and clearer. It was an amazing, joyous feeling, and an experience like no other I had ever had.

Presently, things are not going so well. I vomit several more times, and then stand up and resume shaking my arms and legs and whole body violently. My eyes are closed and my head faces upwards. A feeling of sickness still pervades my being, and I feel that I may need to vomit again shortly. I am whispering the chant over and over again at high speed, "Om Swastiastu Ratu Bagus, Om Swastiastu Ratu Bagus…" and my body is desperately weak and aching. I collapse onto the floor at frequent intervals, but am ushered to my feet by Ratu and his wife who smile and gesture for me to carry on shaking.

I am engaged in the final stages of an intensive five-day 'shaking meditation' retreat with Indian guru and powerhouse Ratu Bagus, and the very foundations of my humanity are being, quite literally, shaken. The routine for the last five days has been thus: wake up at 5am, shake for two hours, breakfast, shake for two hours, lunch, shake for two hours, dinner, shake for two hours, group meditation, sleep (or not, in my case). It has been possibly the most gruelling five days of my life, and on this last day, in this penultimate shaking session, I am really struggling.

The shaking continues. I feel like I can't go on, but force myself to stand up one last time. I begin shaking, and decide to really push myself to 'let go' and force a way through this mental frenzy, somehow. I am now making a wailing sound as saliva dribbles from my mouth, and am screaming more and more loudly in a desperate attempt to trigger some kind of healing process in my body/mind. Something really has to happen soon, I think to myself; I can't take much more than this.

As I find myself collapsing over the vomit bucket once

again, trembling with weakness, I am praying desperately for a similar emotional release to the one that had lifted my spirits several days ago. I simply cannot leave this retreat with my mind in this state. My thoughts are in a total frenzy and my brain aches, such is the mental effort for something to give, for some kind of experience that will bring my mind into peace.

My T-shirt is heavy with sweat as I clamber to my feet *one last time* and begin shaking, although now it is barely a shake, more of a dazed wobble. I have all but given up.

2

George's Cremation Service

September 2004

Rewind two months and I am at St John's Chapel in my home county of Oxfordshire on a crisp, sunny day, attending the funeral of one of my best friends from school, George Whitfield. He has died of a rare muscle cancer, at the age of 23, and we are here for his cremation ceremony.

Many of my old school friends are present, and we mingle around in the grassy area next to the Chapel, catching up a little on what everyone has been up to since we left sixth form. Everyone seems so much older, and yet so much the same. The prettiest girls are still the prettiest girls, and the most intimidating boys still create a fearful presence. But I feel my confidence has increased since the days of sixth form, and in a way feel more mature than many of those with whom I am chatting.

My main memories of George are from the primary school days. We used to spend hours building tunnels of cardboard boxes in my parents' cellar and then crawling through them in the pitch black trying to find whatever objects we had laid down to collect as part of the game, and following the blotches of glow in the dark paint to the prize at the end of the maze. We would spend birthdays together, and I can vividly picture myself sitting in the back of George's mum's car en route to a birthday bowling trip one time. We played football together, went for dinner at each other's house, and were very close friends, if not best friends.

My friendship with George became more distant as we moved up to secondary school, and then into sixth form. We joined different circles of friends and the old sparks that made us best friends were lost in the struggles of being a teenager.

One thing that we continued to have in common was our girlfriends – two of which we shared at different times. One of the girls, Samantha Haywood, a beautiful, lively, outspoken girl, was George's girlfriend all through his battle with cancer and right up to his death. She was also my first proper girlfriend, and my first proper kiss! And before George and Samantha got together there was Melissa May, to whom George always seemed so well suited. She was a very attractive but shy girl, and I was lucky enough to be her boyfriend for a period after she and George split up, though as with so many teenage relationships, it was a fleeting romance.

George always seemed to pick, and win, the most popular girls, most probably because he was a highly likeable, gentle, and thoroughly decent guy.

George's memorial service is about to begin, and a black car pulls up outside the chapel. Out steps Samantha, and it's the first time many of us have seen her since learning of George's passing away. She captures everyone's attention, her hair a striking blonde that contrasts sharply with the redness of her puffy face, damp with tears. She isn't quite sure where to look or how to act, and neither are we. How can we relate to what she must be thinking and feeling right now?

There are so many people gathered to remember George that we don't even nearly fit inside the chapel where the service is taking place. I try to respectfully let others inside first, and eventually take up a position just outside the chapel, with an overflow of around fifteen to twenty others standing around me.

The memorial service is underway, and fond memories of George are recounted. Tears are rolling down my cheeks as I contemplate the agonising beauty that is human life and human death. My mother and grandfather have both passed away in the last year, so death has been a subject never far from my thoughts.

This particular service seems somehow more beautiful than the other memorial services I have attended recently though. Perhaps it is the crispness of the summer's day, or the fact that I am amongst so many people I know. It is a deeply moving occasion, and I am surprised by how comfortable I feel crying in front of my old school friends.

One rather surprising presence at the service is the pop singer and actor Jerome Flynn. Jerome takes a lead role in the service, and it unfolds that George and Jerome became friends whilst engaging in some kind of meditation practice in Bali – something George had been doing in an attempt at healing not long before he died. Jerome talks of George's gentleness and courage, and says what a lively presence he was in such testing circumstances.

The service continues and Samantha walks up to the lectern to speak her eulogy, her constant tears and red face revealing how battered and bruised she is from sharing in George's suffering. She can hardly get the words of her speech out of her mouth, she is crying so much. She makes spontaneous and rehearsed jokes occasionally to try to lighten the mood and the weight of her grief. I feel a certain beauty radiating from her, despite her obvious pain, and I sense that I will always feel that from her.

As Samantha relays her memories of George in small chunks, interspersed with tearful pauses and nose-blows, you can tell she just wants to get the whole thing over with.

3

My Mother's Memorial Service

March 2004

My mother died of an aggressive form of breast cancer in November 2003, a year or so before George passed away. Her illness was complicated by a move away from our family home in Abingdon, Oxfordshire, and back to Holland (where my mother was from) just months before she died. This meant that we organised two memorial services for her, one for her friends and relatives in Holland, followed by one for her English acquaintances.

Due to grief and complicated circumstances it wasn't until March 2004 that we got around to holding the memorial service for my mother in England, but it was well attended by her friends and family. I played a large part in the organisation of the ceremony, enlisting my friend's band to perform, helping choose the venue, organising a sound man and sound system, and constructing an order of service. I had been very close to my mother, and it was important to me that we paid tribute in a way that did justice to all her wonderful qualities.

Watching Samantha read her eulogy at George's cremation ceremony reminded me of when I walked up on stage to read a poem at my mother's English memorial service the previous year. I remember walking slowly up to the microphone with a lump in my throat, and peering down at my trembling hands as I struggled to hold in my tears whilst unfolding a piece of

A4 paper with one of my mother's favourite poems on it.

I placed the piece of paper on the wooden lectern and adjusted the microphone. I glanced up at the room and back down at the page, flattening it with my hand. I told myself in my head to speak loudly and slowly.

I began to read:

> *The same stream of life that runs through my veins night and day*
> *Runs through the world and dances in rhythmic measures.*
> *It is the same life that shoots in joy*
> *Through the dust of the earth into numberless blades of grass*
> *And breaks into tumultuous waves of leaves and flowers.*
> *It is the same life that is rocked in the ocean cradle*
> *Of birth and death, in ebb and in flow.*
> *My limbs are made glorious by the touch of this world of life.*
> *And my pride is from the life-throb of ages*
> *Dancing in my blood this moment.*

I suppose my mother fell in love with that poem because it captures a wonderful sentiment – a single animating life force permeating all things, including birth and death. It is a profound poem, and is testament to the depths of spiritual exploration that she had embarked upon when faced with the imminent likelihood of her death.

George and his mother were in the congregation that day, watching and listening as I read the poem, my voice filled with the muted agony of my mother's death. George's body must have been riddled with cancer as he sat watching. Just as my mother had tried to fight the disease, George was also battling with chemotherapy, special diets, spiritual practices, and more.

My mother and George had actually been in touch a fair amount and become friends before she died. She would drive to visit George and lend him books about spirituality and alternative therapies and healing and hope. The pair were united by their brave efforts in the face of terrible adversity.

But at this time, my mother had lost her battle, and George's battle was still very much alive. And I wonder what was running through George's mind as the sorrowful words of that poem reverberated around that silent, wooden room, as he sat with his own mother watching the memorial service unfold. Was he frightened? Terrified? Defiant?

4

The 'Light' Women

September 2004

George's memorial service drew to a close and an old school friend, Chris Jenkins, offered me a lift back to the home of George's family for the reception. Twenty minutes or so later we pulled up and parked a couple of streets along from the house, got out of the car, and began walking up to the house. Other guests were arriving simultaneously, and I struck up conversation with a short and lively lady who was milling around.

After exchanging greetings, conversation quickly turned to George and how each of us knew him. The lady's name was Priscilla. She told me how George had been on a meditation retreat not long before he died, and that she was a member of the same meditation group of which George, and also Jerome Flynn, had been a part.

We began talking about cancer, and death, and I told her a little about my mother's death and her battle with cancer. She began talking about past lives, a subject that felt quite alien to me, and remarked how George had been trampled upon so much in his past lives that even the powerful shaking meditation he had been doing in Bali wasn't able to save his life.

Priscilla described a spiritual experience that she had been going through recently involving being burned at the stake in a past life. She had been a witch. She had had to undergo torturous witch tests like walking barefoot on hot coals –

it sounded so fictional and so far removed from anything I had ever heard before, and yet she spoke about it with such certainty and reality.

Was I really standing in the presence of a lady who had been a witch in a past life? The thought was quite bewildering, and a little frightening! Priscilla said she'd like to introduce me to a few of her friends. I followed her through George's house into the back garden, where everyone was tucking into sandwiches and drowning memories of George in alcoholic beverages.

Priscilla walked me up to three women who stood together in a semi-circle, eating their lunch. What I saw and felt when I stepped into the presence of these women left me gobsmacked. They seemed to be radiating an immense amount of what I can only describe as light. It was coming from them, and up and around and through them, almost like a force field! And indeed, it forced me to stand rigid with amazement. I had never seen anything like it.

I exchanged the word "amazing" with one of the women, Sally, for some time (maybe we were amazed by a kind of connection we were all experiencing), and I was so shocked by what was happening that I didn't know where to look, or what to think!

"Wow!" said Sally enthusiastically, as we stood looking into each other's eyes, "a kindred spirit, for sure!" I took these words to be a great compliment, and they lodged firmly in my mind. Perhaps it was a boost to my self-esteem to think that I might be associated with these light-wielding women, and may even be a light-wielding person myself! (In spiritual circles there is so much talk of light and enlightenment, and I was truly fascinated by the idea that I might somehow become enlightened.)

I got talking to these 'light' women about my mother and about my background with George, and they told me about the shaking meditation they were doing, and how it was a wonderful and powerful way of removing emotional blockages. What they said held resonance with me, as through my mother's battle with cancer I had explored the links between emotional and physical disease in some depth. My mother had introduced me to various proponents of Eastern alternative therapies, Deepak Chopra in particular, with his philosophy that drew on accessing deeper levels of oneself through meditation as a source of healing.

Sally said that there was a shaking meditation group in London and that I should come along. It all sounded very exciting! She handed me a small card with a picture of a well-built longhaired Indian man on the front and the words 'Om Swastiastu Ratu Bagus'. She explained that Ratu was the leader of this shaking meditation practice, and that he had led the retreats in Bali that George attended not long before he died.

Later that evening I went for dinner in a local restaurant with a group of old school friends who had been at the ceremony that day. I tried to engage with the light-hearted conversations about what everyone had been up to and how we all were, but my mind kept flicking back to the 'light' women I had met at the reception, and the shaking practice they had told me about, and the picture of Ratu that I had tucked away in my bag. I was looking forward to the bus journey back home to London that night, when I could be on my own at last to chew over the experiences of the day, and ponder what the significance of my introduction to Ratu Bagus might be.

5

My Mother's Illness

2000–2003

In 2003 my mother finally left my father and our family home in Abingdon to move to Holland and go solo on her healing journey. Her battle with breast cancer had already been going on for over two years, and she had gone through at least three different types of chemotherapy, lost all her hair, had a cancerous breast removed, seen her marriage fall apart, lost much of the feeling in her fingers and toes (from the chemotherapy), had her upper spine targeted intensely with radiotherapy, had radio frequency ablation on her liver, and general suffered a frightening amount at the hands of this relentless disease.

Of course, with cancer, it's not just the treatment and its torturous side effects, it's also the countless visits to the hospital, meetings with doctors and consultants, the waiting rooms, the fearful car journeys, and everything else that comes along with being ill with this serious disease.

I would try to accompany my mother on her hospital visits whenever I could. It was always especially saddening for me when she came home alone after her latest set of results and there was more bad news – the cancer had spread again. She would have to tell us the bad news, usually with tears in her eyes and a broken heart.

My mother was a tennis enthusiast, and also loved her hobbies of sewing and cooking, but the sickness that she felt with a fresh dose of chemotherapy running through her blood and internal organs left her with practically no energy. She would sit in an armchair in our front room, turned to face the telly and staring blankly at it, feeling sick and weak for hours on end.

She would sit with her head angled slightly forward from all of the radiotherapy that had been targeted to the spread of cancer at the top of her spine, and with a rug draped over her lap for comfort. I would walk over to her and give her a hug now and again, and sit on the floor beside her legs. I would offer her drinks of green tea (rich in anti-oxidants), make her hot water bottles to hold, and do anything I could to help comfort her suffering a little.

What despair, fear, upset, degradation, and helplessness must she have experienced through this period of terrible suffering. But she desperately wanted to get better, and as she would remark to us on frequent occasions, she was going to fight it.

6

Family Breakdown

2000–2003

My mother was diagnosed with cancer in the winter of 2000. I returned home late one evening from the pub, where I had been drinking with friends and teachers after a school open day. I was in the sixth form at the time, and it wasn't so unusual for teachers and students to be socialising together as we were now young adults.

I was ushered into the kitchen where the whole family was gathered and my mother broke the news to me. It was clearly a very traumatic announcement to have to make, and her voice was full of fear and sadness as she spoke.

The announcement followed a long period of friction in my parents' relationship, and it was clear that my mother held a lot of resentment towards my father regarding the way in which their relationship had fallen apart. She didn't like the way he treated my sister and me, and she didn't like the way he treated her.

I remember that as we all stood together in the kitchen that night after my mother broke the news, my father brought us into an uncomfortable family hug – perhaps he was hoping that this dramatic turn of events would be the catalyst for positive change in the family, when healing would take place after a period of breakdown.

But as it turned out, the opposite was true. For months, a feeling of misery clouded over our family life. The tension between my parents was at times unbearable.

Mealtimes were particularly uncomfortable. We would eat largely in silence, and the moment my mother had finished her meal she would angle herself away from my father to avoid eye contact with him. My sister was away at university, but I generally sat right in the middle between the two of them. My mother would often comment to me how she hated my father's staring eyes, and it was obvious she felt seriously intimidated by his presence.

Then there were the arguments. These generally took place towards the end of the evening after dinner, though they happened at any time of the day. My parents would close the dining room door and speak in Dutch in an effort to shield our ears from their angry exchanges; but that did little to stop the hurt and the anger penetrating the walls of the house and entering into our consciousness.

They began sleeping in separate rooms and family communications became increasingly strained until that fateful time when my mother made up her mind that she could take the strain no more and had to leave.

I have a vivid picture in my mind of my father's reaction as my mother said goodbye on the day that she left for Holland. He cried loudly and with a manic desperation that sounded partly forced – perhaps he didn't know how he *should* be acting at this time of great change and despair for our family. The only time I had ever heard my father cry like this (or at all) was after he had heard the news that his mother had died alone of a heart attack a few years earlier.

Moments before my mother left, she and my father stood facing each other in the small hallway leading towards the front door. My mother looked terribly guilty and painfully sad, and didn't react to my father's attempts at a goodbye hug and kiss. She just looked all around, avoiding his gaze, and battling with the emotional distress of the situation.

The indescribable guilt she must have felt about the crumbling of our family was there in her face, and I felt it as a terror in my body as I hurriedly went around loading up the car, checking the oil level, preparing a packed lunch, and doing anything I could to lighten the burden of this traumatic experience for my mother and for myself.

This was the end of the family unit my father had struggled so hard to preserve for many years. His sense of Christian morality had led him to fight back against divorce attempts from my mother, who had made a long list of accusations against him that her lawyer had actually deemed worthy of grounds for divorce. But she could never quite go through with the divorce proceedings. I think it was just too hard for her; to deal with the fighting, the cancer, the divorce proceedings, and the repercussions for the family.

7

First Shaking Session

October 2004

Sally, one of the 'light' women from George's memorial service who had given me the card depicting Ratu Bagus, also supplied me with a phone number for Jeremy, who was the facilitator of a shaking meditation group that met in Herne Hill, not all that far from where I was living and working in South West London.

I spoke to Jeremy on the phone, and it was a brief factual conversation in which he invited me along to a 'shaking' session, told me to bring some old clothes, some music if I wished, and informed me of how to get to the Lido in Herne Hill where the practice took place.

As I arrived at the Lido for my first shaking session I was both anxious and excited, and after looking around the building for a few minutes I entered a medium-sized, square room, where music was playing from one end next to a large banner depicting Ratu Bagus. A few people stood facing the banner, holding their arms out in front of them and shaking their bodies at various different speeds.

Jeremy came and greeted me and I asked him what I was supposed to do! He laughed and gave me few instructions; he simply advised that I should stand and start to shake and let 'the energy' guide me.

I walked into a space, stood facing the banner, and did as

Jeremy had instructed. I lifted my arms in front of me, and slowly but surely began shaking. I didn't exactly experience the 'fireworks' that I was maybe expecting from a practice like this, but I was determined to give the practice a real go, so I persevered. I found myself quite spontaneously adopting strange yogic postures, leaning over at certain angles and falling to the floor at times. Was this 'the energy' in some way moving through me?

Towards the end of the session the energy in the room grew, the shaking intensified, and a kind of climax was reached, with people wailing and shouting and chanting and shaking. After the session reached its energetic peak, the music was faded down, and the room began to slow its movements, with individuals ceasing shaking and slowly dropping to the floor and to their knees, and lying forward with heads to the ground, all facing the banner of Ratu. People sighed and long out-breaths could be heard as each person settled into a place of peace. I was simply relieved that I had survived this first shaking session unharmed, so I just followed what the others were doing.

After a few minutes of quiet, one of the group leaders ushered everyone to the front of the room where a seated circle was formed, and a general discussion took place. People discussed forthcoming events, retreats, significant goings-on in their lives, magical experiences, and whatever else came to mind. It was perhaps the most 'sane' part of the evening!

When the group discussion drew to a close the session was over, and everyone went to the back of the room to get changed out of their shaking clothes and get ready, presumably, to return to whatever kind of lives these people were leading. I struck up conversation with a few people, and it certainly seemed that all had normal jobs and were leading normal lives. Several of the 'light' women I had met at George's memorial service were there, so it almost felt as though I was amongst friends.

I left that first shaking session with a mixture of emotions, but on the whole I felt it had been a positive experience, and I wanted to know more about why all these people were dedicated to this practice and what I could get out of it! For many months I had been preoccupied by a feeling that I was carrying around some kind of illness in my body, and although I had no idea what that illness was, and there was no evidence at all that I was unwell, I felt that I needed serious healing of some kind in order to be whole and healthy. Perhaps this practice would provide the feeling of wellbeing I had been striving for.

I continued to attend the shaking sessions on a weekly basis, and every week brought different experiences. As I grew in confidence, the shaking became more intense, and I would find myself doing strange things like gently hitting different parts of my body. I also became aware of other dimensions to the practice through talking to the others.

At certain points during a session, people would line up on the left hand side of the room, where one person would stand with a syringe. The syringe, it transpired, contained a tobacco solution created especially by Ratu, and I was told that this solution represented 'light energy' and was very cleansing to the body. Each person in the queue received a shot of the solution up his or her nose. I noticed people had been vomiting in the toilets during the session – was this all part of them cleansing their bodies of disease? As eager as I was for healing to take place in my own body and mind, I was very afraid to try squirting this substance up my nose and so I stayed focused on the shaking and left the tobacco solution to the 'experts'!

Every week, during the talk time at the end of the session, people would mention forthcoming retreats. The date for one such retreat was approaching quickly; it was only weeks way. "You MUST go on the retreat!" I would be told repeatedly by various different people each week – it would mean I would get to meet Ratu in person and apparently this was when the most amazing healing and spiritual experiences took place.

It was a real struggle for me deciding whether or not to attend the retreat in Devon in November 2004. But I believed that I was carrying around some kind of disease, and I was very lost spiritually. I was willing to try anything that might enlighten me, stabilise me, and give me some peace of mind. After weeks of procrastination, with a certain nervous excitement, I booked my place on the retreat.

8

My Mother's Final Days

November 2003

The last few days of my mother's life were quite something. I graduated from university only three or so days before my mother passed away. I remember leaving the graduation ceremony in London and immediately preparing to board a plane to Holland. My mother was so proud of me for achieving a first class degree, and was so very eager to attend the ceremony. It was perhaps her last wish, and it was a terrible shame that she was far too ill to fly to England.

For the previous few months I had been flying back and forth between England and Holland on an almost weekly basis, wanting to spend as much time with my mother as possible. But I had also landed my first proper job, working for a prestigious group of record labels in the heart of the music industry in London – it was a fantastic opportunity and I decided to pursue that position rather than move to Holland to live with my mother. In retrospect the decision seems somewhat selfish, but it is probably what she would have wanted and she was still very much determined that she would recover from her illness.

But this time, when I boarded the plane after the graduation ceremony, it was a one-way ticket. My mother's prognosis meant that her prospects were very bleak, and being the closest person she had in the world I naturally wanted to spend every moment possible with her.

*

In the final days of her life my mother lost a great deal of weight, became very pale, and was totally bed-ridden. She refused to go to the hospital – she wanted to die at home. And if things got really bad, she wanted to use euthanasia to end her life. This was in fact one of the main reasons she had moved back to Holland, rather than moving to another part of England to battle with the disease.

Since moving back to Holland my mother had been on an alternative therapy diet called the Gerson therapy which entailed a daunting routine of fruit and vegetable juices (in huge quantities) and coffee enemas throughout the day, and little else for nourishment. The routine was very demanding, requiring a special hand-operated juicer to be used in conjunction with various other tools, and my mother even had a special reverse-osmosis water machine to give extra purity to all that she was consuming. She would also dedicate periods of time each day to meditation, aware as she was of stories about spontaneous remissions and the healing power that could be found in advanced meditative states.

Her willingness to embark on such a gruelling routine was testament to her courage and her ceaseless desire to recover. But sadly, the diet produced little in the way of encouraging results and there reached a point when, it would be fair to say, my mother gave up.

In her final days my mother could eat only grapes and slices of melon, and subsequently became very weak, though she struggled to maintain a routine and her dignity by insisting on taking a shower and putting on some make-up each day. She would always make sure that my sister and I had something to drink, and was still trying to take care of us right up until her death. She was a brave woman.

Every available space in my mother's small bedroom was filled with beautiful bunches of flowers – gifts from friends, relatives, and old colleagues.

As her condition deteriorated my mother would vomit regularly, and I assisted her by emptying and washing out her sick bucket on each occasion. She began to sleep more and more, and in the final couple of days of her life she needed around-the-clock care, which I provided.

In her final hours, my mother was very uncomfortable. She was clearly experiencing nightmares, and she was on an adjustable bed which she kept asking to be adjusted up and down so that she could lie a little more comfortably. Not long before she died, she lost control of her bodily functions, and I cleared up the mess with whatever towels I could find. This was no longer a time for dignity.

My mother's nightmares intensified and she requested for the euthanasia doctor to be called, saying "I don't think I've got long left". Indeed, she didn't have long at all, and within the next half hour she made a final adjustment, and with a loud death rattle drew her last breaths before the euthanasia doctor was even on his way.

9

Returning from the Retreat

November 2004

Having left the shaking meditation retreat in Devon a session early due to my body and mind being in such an awful state, I took a train back to London where I was living in a shared house with four of my student friends. I was studying an undergraduate degree at the University of Westminster, though for some months my attentions had been focused far more on spiritual things than academic things.

On the journey home I sat next to Gary who had also been on the retreat, but our relative dispositions were in stark contrast. Gary spoke excitedly about how he hoped to one day have his own taman (tent) for shaking, and as we journeyed along he made notes about his plans for the future and generally seemed invigorated and enthused by the retreat experience. I, on the other hand, felt awful – lost, confused, and depressed in a way I can hardly attempt to describe.

I remember when our train arrived at London Paddington and Gary and I exchanged farewells. He could obviously see how traumatised I had been by the shaking experience and wanted to offer me some reassurance. "Big family!" he emphasised to me repeatedly – "We're a big family!"

As I got on the tube back to North West London I was heavily in thought, full of confusion, upset, fear, anger – all in a mess. I was deeply depressed, and felt like there was nowhere in the world I could turn for help. Who could really understand what I had been through and was going through? Shaking meditation isn't your everyday thing, after all.

I arrived home and spent a little time trying to explain my feelings and what had been happening to my housemates John and Louise. John remarked that I looked terrible, and I became aware that I had lost a lot of weight through my shaking ordeal. I tried talking about the retreat, trying to express what this shaking practice was all about, but struggled to communicate my experiences in a way that resonated with the two of them.

The following days did little to alleviate the depression I was experiencing. It really did feel like there was no way out of this dark state of mind, and I would spend hours lying in bed, hiding under the sheets, feeling totally messed up.

A few days after returning from the retreat I spoke to my friend Tony on the phone, and I communicated to him how much I was struggling. Tony was keen to help and had some interesting and unusual advice to offer. He told me, quite simply, to ask myself the question "who am I?" and *feel* the response. I did as he said, and on my first attempt had the experience of a deeper part of myself coming to the surface, pushing through all the mess of my mind, and bringing me instead to a place of greater feeling, clarity and peace. This gave me great hope! It was like the light I was looking for.

Tony instructed me further to cling to the feeling 'I', and this became my constant practice over the following weeks. And whenever I held this feeling, a feeling of *being*, I felt safe. When I got distracted, however, the depression would set back in. Particularly in the morning when I awoke, and in my dreams, all of the depressive muddle would come back up to the surface.

Through spiritual explorations in the past I had come to an understanding that 'my thoughts are not me', and I had experienced several glimpses of what I believed to be *the real me* at earlier moments in my life.

I remember, for instance, a feeling of great excitement as I sat in the car, driving from London to visit my parents in Abingdon, during my second year as a student. I was listening to a Deepak Chopra tape that my mother had given me, and he was talking about different levels of consciousness, about the body being a powerful pharmacy, and about the infinite possibilities of reality – it all seemed so true and so exciting and really resonated with me.

On other occasions, at home in our shared student house in North London, I used to sit in the bath for hours listening to talks by the comparative religion philosopher Alan Watts as he talked about the different religions of the world and how they were all expressions of the same universal truths. I would sit in my room meditating sometimes, and would get occasional glimpses of feelings of great love or 'self', though they would only last a second or two before my heavily analytical mind would kick in and excitedly try to analyse the experience.

I remember one such similar experience when I was in Holland visiting my mother during her illness. I was in bed with my eyes closed, allowing stillness to settle in my mind, and I felt an amazing feeling of expanding awareness and bliss. I tried to describe it to my mother in the hope that she was experiencing the same thing in her own meditation efforts, and she said she was but looked rather confused, so I'm not sure she really knew what I was describing.

Another time I was meditating in a different student

house in North London, and I reached such a deep place of meditation that I felt my bodily form dissolve into a feeling of bliss! In Hindu culture they call this experience Sat-Chit-Ananda (or Existence Consciousness Bliss), and experiencing this was a pivotal moment in my life. It was like a deep and profound realisation that who I was, my nature, was not my body. I immediately texted my friend Tony, who I believed to be a master of such practices, to tell him the good news!

Another such enlightening experience was when I took Ecstasy for the first time. The feeling of truth and understanding was amazing, I really was in ecstasy, and miracles were happening before my eyes.

One such miraculous experience took place on a bus. I was with a girl called Cathy that I had met at a music industry party that night. I felt that I was totally in love with her. I was basking in feelings of ecstasy, and she was attempting to direct us back to my house but struggling to get me to focus on the practical matter of buses and directions, such was my absorption in the joy and beauty I was experiencing.

We finally got on the right bus, but it was completely full, with every seat taken and people standing everywhere. We walked upstairs to look for space but it was just as full, so we walked back downstairs again. At the bottom of the stairs, right in front of us, two free seats had miraculously appeared, though no one had moved and the bus hadn't stopped. I couldn't believe my eyes! We laughed as we went over to the seats and sat down. I felt that somehow those seats had magically been made free for us, though I didn't know how. The sceptic will claim there are obvious explanations for what happened, but for me at that time it was a really miraculous happening!

For several days after that first experience of Ecstasy I felt a deep peace and clarity, and I knew it was a hugely significant event in my life. I was so much calmer in my relationships with people, and everything seemed so much easier. The trivialities of life seemed much less important than before.

All of these spiritual experiences contributed to an awareness that there is more to reality than the mundane, and more to being alive than the everyday thoughts and feelings that form our common experience. The glimpses of meditative bliss and ecstasy that I experienced pointed to something deeper and more profound at the heart of the mystery of life.

10

Spiritual Exploration

Winter 2003

Back to 2003, and having returned from the shaking meditation retreat and caught a glimpse of my deeper self through my friend Tony's advice of clinging to the feeling 'I', my hope and faith had been restored. This newly discovered practice was like a signpost that pointed to a place of clarity.

But as I was to discover is so often the case with Eastern meditation practices, doubt, frustration, and uncertainty surfaced and I found myself experiencing very depressed and disturbed states of mind. My friends tried to help me but I felt that their own problems were such that they weren't helping me – really, without meaning it, they were simply adding to my confusion.

My days were spent going backward and forward between desperate depression and the relief and clarity I felt when I sat alone in my room, clinging to the feeling, 'I'. Tony suggested that I read a book by Indian spiritual master Sri Ramana Maharshi, *Be As You Are*, which I read every day and found to be a compelling and constant reminder of what I then believed to be 'the truth'. Every line in the book resonated with me, and I was so grateful to have discovered it.

During these days and weeks I would sit on my bed, or in parks, or walk along the streets of North London, reading passages from that book, and feeling a sense of understanding and truth as I did so. But the desperation persisted, and I was still plagued by the uncomfortable experiences of the shaking meditation retreat, and was seeking for someone to help me.

I was very sceptical of doctors (at this time I was focused much more on Eastern therapies and remedies than those of the West – most probably as a result of witnessing the horrors of the cancer treatment my mother had recently undergone), but I reluctantly agreed to see my GP, and I struggled to explain about the shaking meditation and the mess it had left me in, without any sense I could communicate with him in a meaningful way about this. My GP proceeded to prescribe me some kind of anti-depressants, but I wasn't happy to take them. The prescription remained in my desk drawer and I looked instead for alternative sources of help and comfort.

My girlfriend Louise suggested I could try speaking to the vicar from her hometown, a gentleman called Rob. She said he was a very peaceful chap who had done lots of meditation and might be able to help me. I phoned Rob and we talked things through. It was a conversation that gave me some reassurance, but it wasn't the life changing help I was looking for at that time.

My sister suggested that I speak to her friend Janine's mother, a Jewish lady who my sister informed me was very spiritual and might be able to help me. I spoke with Janine's mother and she told me about a spiritual counsellor who she had been to see and whom she highly recommended. I was a little sceptical about the idea of attending a talking therapy, but I was keen to try anything and so I got in touch with him right away and arranged to meet up for a session.

In my first and only session with the spiritual counsellor I began to talk about my experiences with the shaking meditation, but the response I got from the counsellor was not encouraging. The feeling and atmosphere both of him and his surroundings didn't resonate with me, and I left with a view to perhaps going back, but thinking mainly about how quiet he was, how confused he looked, and how much he was charging!

So I was still on my own, and still searching.

At the worst times during this period following the shaking meditation retreat I would be holding so much fear and emotional pain in my body that I would feel as though my heart was going to give up. The feelings of fear running through my body were sometimes so intense and horrendous that I would vomit. The dreams that I experienced would leave me terrified to go to sleep.

11

Ramana Maharshi Meditation Retreat

March 2005

Still searching for that elusive enlightenment, that peace of mind, I arranged to attend a Sri Ramana Maharshi meditation retreat in Kent, which attracted me because it seemed more peaceful and gentle than the shaking meditation retreat led by Ratu Bagus that I had been on several months before. The memory of that retreat still tormented me, but this was something rather different.

The retreat took place in a farmhouse in the Kent countryside, and about eight people were in attendance. There were regular, healthy meals in a comfortable environment, and the spiritual practice that was the focus of the retreat was not emotionally or physically demanding.

Although meditation and the practice of self-enquiry (the 'who am I?' practice that Tony had taught me) formed part of the retreat, the laid-back approach meant that there was much more casual discussion about the practice than engagement with the practice itself. I found this to be very frustrating. After all, I was truly seeking enlightenment; I didn't want to talk about it!

To my mind, the retreat was focusing much too much on the intellectual understanding of self-enquiry, rather than dedicating time to the practice itself. To discuss enquiry in an abstract way is one thing, but to actually involve oneself in the practice is another. I became frustrated that people seemed to be enjoying relaxing and eating good food rather than getting stuck into the spiritual aspects of the retreat.

But the experience was a valuable one. It is always interesting to see how others go about their meditation practices, and the group meditation sessions were enjoyable, even if they did only last for 20-30 minutes at a time, which was comparatively easy-going compared to the practices I was more used to.

As well as the meditation sessions we dabbled in some yoga, spoke about sacred geometry, and spent some time in an enclosure at the bottom of the garden in which there was a multicoloured-light-emitting device that presumably had some spiritual significance that was (and still is) alien to me!

On the last day of the Ramana Maharshi meditation retreat, the subject of satsang was being discussed. I wasn't sure what satsang was, and I was told it is a question and answer session with a guru. The owners of the farmhouse where the retreat was being hosted were giving away videos of satsang with various spiritual gurus, including Gangaji and Papaji.

Papaji had been a disciple of Sri Ramana Maharshi, and Gangaji had been a disciple of Papaji. One of the guys on the retreat, Sam, said that he went to satsang with a fellow called Mooji, who was an enlightened disciple of Papaji. Mooji gave satsang twice a week in Brixton, which was conveniently just a short journey from where I lived in London.

Sam gave me Mooji's website address, and I took videos of Gangaji and Papaji away with me – these all felt like things I wanted to investigate as I continued to pursue spiritual enlightenment.

12

Satsang With Mooji

May 2005

When I returned from the Ramana Maharshi meditation retreat in Kent, the first thing I wanted to do was watch the Gangaji and Papaji videos. They were instantly inspiring, and I got a real sense that the gurus were speaking from a place of truth. I enjoyed watching them, and at times laughed out loud along with the gurus at the seemingly insane questioning of the spiritual seekers, but when I switched off the videos I always found myself sitting with a feeling of confusion about how all of this related to my own 'enlightenment'.

Awkward questions flooded my mind. What exactly is enlightenment? Is it something that can happen gradually, or must it happen in an instant? Was I already enlightened, perhaps, and if so would I be asking these questions? The gurus say there is no enlightenment, and yet at times they say that the realisation of who you are can happen in an instant – aren't these two statements contradictory? Which is true?

Is this instantaneous realisation something that has already happened to me, like when Tony told me to feel 'I' and I felt a strong sense of being come to the surface, or is it a new experience that I am still awaiting? What am I missing here? Is it possible to be enlightened and confused simultaneously? Or would my enlightenment be a moment still to come that would eliminate my confusion and suffering forever?

I decided that I would go and see Mooji, and experience

this satsang for the first time. Maybe he would be able to shed light on some of these awkward questions. I looked on his website, and his writing resonated with a feeling of truth in me, so it felt right that I should go along.

Mooji gave satsang in the living room of his ground floor flat in Brixton on Wednesday and Sunday nights. It was a cramped little room that fitted in about 15 or so spiritual seekers. I arrived a little late one Wednesday, at about 7.10pm, and the front room was already full, so I was forced to sit just outside the doorway in the narrow corridor that led to Mooji's bathroom.

I saw Sam, the chap from the meditation retreat in Kent who had told me about Mooji, said a quiet hello, and sat down beside him so that I could just about see into the front room. Mooji was sitting on a large armchair with a white throw covering his legs, and was facing towards the room. The seekers were all either cross-legged on the floor, on one of two sofas against the back and side walls, or leaning back against walls and furniture.

The burning of incense, candles, and oil burners gave the flat a mystical aroma. The walls were adorned with pictures of India, of Papaji, of Sri Ramana Maharshi and of other spiritual figures. Gentle, Indian pipe music was playing softly in the background. The atmosphere was very still despite the large number of people cramped into such a small space. Everyone sat in silence, though a loud jangle would interrupt the silence every time a late arrival entered Mooji's front door.

Mooji's head boasted long dreadlocks, and his appearance was close to my stereotypical image of a Rastafarian. He put his hands on his knees and began slowly casting his eyes around the room, reacting differently to each person as they met his gaze. With some people he would look solemn and straight-faced and nod gently, with others he would smile deeply and even begin to laugh a little, while nodding with happy approval.

I felt rather nervous – how would he react when he looked at me? How would I react? I sat still looking into Mooji's eyes, and attempting to gage what exactly it was that this man had to offer.

His gazing at each person continued. I grew more nervous as his gaze approached the area where I was sitting. As his eyes met mine, he smiled deeply and gave a little wave, which I took to mean, "Hello! Welcome." I felt a pang of panic as he looked at me – can he see how nervous and insecure I am feeling in this alien environment? Does that demonstrate my unenlightenedness?! Should I try and look as peaceful as possible so he doesn't realise I'm nervous? But surely if he is enlightened he is going to see straight through that!

I settled down a little as I absorbed Mooji's warm smile, and felt a calm presence exuding from him. As his eyes left mine and moved on to the next seeker, I relaxed and sank back into a more comfortable pose. I concentrated on feeling Mooji's presence, and trying to gage how different he was, if at all, to anyone else I had ever met.

When he had taken a good look at everyone in the room, Mooji put his hands together and said "OK, Om, welcome to Satsang", the "Om" coinciding with a bow of his head to the room. Everyone echoed the Om gesture back to Mooji, some saying Om in return, some staying silent. Everyone relaxed and adjusted their position a little. Mooji then invited people to present their questions, and a question and answer session unfolded.

*

During a regular satsang at Mooji's place people asked questions about feelings they were experiencing, or areas of confusion that they felt. Mooji's responses were different according to who was asking the question and the question posed, but every answer was similar in one respect. Mooji would always conclude by asking the questioner to look for who it is that is asking the question. "Find him and bring him to me," he would say, in reference to the fact that there is nothing that you can grab hold of with your mind that *is* yourself. The whole of satsang with Mooji could be summarised as an investigation into the question "who am I?", or perhaps more subtly, "what am I referring to when I say 'I'?"

So, various problems were presented, and Mooji persisted in pointing each and every person back to him- or herself in different ways. I considered that I might ask Mooji a question – a few sprang to mind – but I felt so nervous that I thought this would be my observing satsang, and perhaps next time I might muster up the courage to ask a question.

After about another hour or so Mooji signalled the end of the session by saying thank you and "Om", and gesturing again with his hands together and a bow of the head. The closing Om gesture was echoed by the congregation in a staggered unison, and then Mooji requested that an announcement be read out. The announcement served to keep order in the cramped room as a transition was made to the more relaxed part of the evening.

Mooji then made his way into the adjacent kitchen where he began to prepare several large pots of chai (Indian spiced tea). While he was doing this, the seekers prepared the room for 'chai time' by laying down mats and rugs, onto which were placed an array of chocolates and biscuits and cakes that people had brought. It was a laid back and enjoyable end to proceedings, and there was a warm and friendly atmosphere.

My general understanding of what was going on in satsang is this. When people like Mooji ask you "what is 'I'?" it is a way of focusing attention inward, towards yourself (your real self/'the self'). The aim is to expose the unrealities that sit in us as abstract ideas about ourselves and about the present. Anything that one talks about with reference to 'I' or relationships with people is the past, and the past only exists as an idea. By exposing these things in satsang we are pointed towards what is not merely an idea (what is not the past), and that is the present moment where peace (and enlightenment?) can be found.

I continued to attend satsang with Mooji for a few months, but I found the experience largely unhelpful in terms of my spiritual struggle. I continued to be mentally distressed and the peace and stability I was searching for was still proving to be elusive.

13

Psychotherapy With Peter

2005 – 2007

I have some quite vivid memories of being at the Glastonbury Arts Festival with my friend Tony and my girlfriend Louise in the summer of 2005, and feeling as though I couldn't enjoy the vibrancy of the festival due to being preoccupied with terrible emotional states that I was experiencing.

I remember having the sense that my body was filled with negative energy or disease, and that I simply had to 'get it out of me' somehow. I was having the most awful dreams. I recall that in one dream in particular one of my mother's eyes was sliced open and blood was pouring out. I would also picture her in advanced cancerous states, and the intensity of the dreams was staggering. It was now several years since my mother had passed away, but I was clearly still haunted by the suffering she had endured.

Milling around the festival I spent a lot of time in the healing fields, looking for some kind of therapy that might release me from my suffering. I tried one particular practice where I lay down on my back, and the practitioner moved her hands over my body pressing gently in certain areas. She particularly focused on the abdomen area, which is where I felt I was holding a lot of emotional pain. I presume she was aiming to detect blockages and transfer some kind of healing energy to me.

The practice left me feeling largely unsatisfied, and I

continued wandering around the festival with Tony, trying to stay positive (and he was very encouraging), but feeling so unhappy – I didn't know what else to try!

In one conversation with Tony, he casually slipped into the conversation "Have you tried psychotherapy?" and I responded that I hadn't. It sounded very 'Western' to me. It transpired that Tony had been in psychotherapy for several years, and I suppose it was the strength of character I felt from him that made me take his question seriously.

When the festival was over, I returned home and focused my attentions on investigating how to begin psychotherapy. I was keen to work with the same therapist as Tony, as in terms of spiritual peace and knowledge Tony seemed to have something that I didn't, but that I desired.

I went for an initial assessment at the Chiron Centre for Psychotherapy in London, and conveyed in a very real way (with frequent tearful outbursts) my obsession with enlightenment and my desire for my suffering to ease and for my spirit to find peace.

Fortunately, I was referred to Peter Endlesham, the therapist who had been working with Tony for the last couple of years. It felt like a huge relief, and when I spoke to Peter on the phone he seemed down to earth and self-assured. I had great hope, and I arranged for an initial appointment as soon as possible.

The first time I met with Peter I was instantly impressed. He radiated a kind of light and had an assured but kind demeanour, and within about the first thirty seconds of the meeting I became convinced he could help me. Peter was a 'body psychotherapist', which appealed to me because of my interest in Eastern alternative therapies that worked with emotional blockages in the body.

We spoke for five or ten minutes and then Peter asked me to stand up and go over to a different part of the room, where he told me to crouch down and press my back against the wall, and breathe. I suppose that through this activity Peter was trying to make me feel a sense of the solid, the real, in contrast to the mess of emotions that I was experiencing.

Next, I stood up, and Peter held my arms out in front of me. He once again told me to breathe deeply, and I sensed that somehow he was working with energies in me in a way that I didn't understand. I felt a strange rush of energy and then began to almost hyperventilate, at which point Peter pointed out that we should stop and return to the seats on the other side of the room. Something significant was certainly going on, and I felt that I trusted Peter, and decided I would keep seeing him.

On the whole my sessions with Peter consisted of talking therapy focused around my mother. I would frequently burst into tears, and I had the genuine feeling that I was indeed working through emotional blockages, and that crying was a way of releasing those blockages. In a way that I can't describe, Peter seemed to ask just the right questions at the right time, triggering a response in me that always surprised me, moved me, and helped me enormously.

I continued to see Peter on a weekly basis for nearly two years. It was a tremendous support and I felt my whole character develop in a really positive way. I became aware of childhood tendencies that I was still hanging on to, and I learned to walk around with a sense of self-esteem and confidence – with my head held high!

This was the first time since my mother became ill in 2000 that I had a sense of being on top of things and of being able to cope with the world. Life was still presenting challenges, as no doubt it always will. But with the opportunity to have an hour of Peter's attention devoted to me each week, with his life experience and emotional expertise, I was growing in a positive way and was stronger and more stable than I had been for many years.

But, as I was to become acutely aware of in time, there are powers that are far greater than a psychotherapist in this world, and I was about to face a new set of challenges that would change my perception of reality forever.

14

Psychotic Episodes

2007 and 2009

While psychotherapy was an invaluable support to me and helped me to come to terms with years of depression and emotional distress, unfortunately it didn't stop my mental state at times becoming disturbed and abnormal.

On two occasions during my adult years I have had episodes of experience that have been termed by medical professionals, 'psychosis'. It is worth bearing in mind that the experiences I had during these two 'episodes' were very different, although there are in some ways similarities between them.

The first thing that I wish to point out is that I am no longer experiencing psychosis. Both times that I experienced this condition I ended up in hospital (I will talk more about how that came to be the case), and was treated. I am happy to say that for a long time now my thoughts have been very much down to earth and clear, and I experience a healthy, normal state of mind – as far as there is such a thing!

I am still having regular check-ups with medical professionals, so it would be fair to say that if I were to relapse, there would be recognisable warning signs that would crop up – indicators that would help to keep me safe from harm and from harming others.

In contemporary society it is typical to talk of one's past in terms of a chronological history, and it would be possible for me to recall my psychotic episodes in this way. However, I wish to talk in more general terms about my experience of psychosis, drawing on the similarities that I experienced between the two episodes, recalling certain experiences, and trying to convey in an easily understandable way what psychosis is.

In an open and honest conversation with my CPN (Community Psychiatric Nurse) Anthony in Oxfordshire one time in 2007, I was asked what it had been like to experience psychosis. A straightforward question you might think, but this was the one and only time I had ever been asked this by a medical professional, and it was not an easy question to answer.

I struggled to find words to describe what for the most part had been fragmentary and disjointed experiences. I said to Ashley that I had felt like I was in a computer game. That I, in certain respects, became like a character in a grand play that was so lifelike that it was in fact my life. These two analogies capture something of what it is like to experience psychosis.

One element of the psychosis I experienced is fantasy. During one of my episodes I developed a complex fantasy in relation to a particular shop and its staff. I went into this shop every day for several weeks, and became somehow obsessed with a girl who worked in the shop. I might add that this was not a dark obsession (although you could possibly perceive it to be that way if you have seen enough scary movies!) but it was rather more light-hearted in character. I would buy certain products from time to time as a way of interacting with the girl, which is perhaps not so psychotic. But then I would write her letters, letters that were imbued with complex hidden sexual meanings. I used a £100 Parker pen and expensive paper to compose these letters, and at one time I was writing her a letter a day! I made a compilation CD of upbeat love songs and took it in to the shop for her. I even bought her a goldfish, though she wasn't in the shop when I tried to deliver it to her, so I ended up keeping it.

Although not behaving in a way that could be considered dangerous, I did cross certain boundaries of regular behaviour, and very much regret acting in the way that I did. I later apologised to the shop manager and to all the staff for any upset or distress that I had caused.

During that particular psychotic episode, letter writing in general was my big obsession. I developed a deep and profound love for putting pen to paper, and I would write a few letters a day, to different people. Some I would tear up and throw away, others I would post in various post boxes in the area surrounding where I lived. I used to walk around my neighbourhood for hours on end looking for new post boxes rather than simply posting the letters in the post box closest to where I lived. I can't explain why I did this, but I derived a certain pleasure from walking. I always wore the same tweed jacket and top hat when going on these long letter-posting walks – it was a rather Dickensian look, and perhaps a little unusual, but I loved the outfit and wore it with pride.

Another one of the unfortunate recipients of my letters was the Chair of Philosophy at Oxford University. I wrote to him often, conveying my passion for and understanding of philosophy with word games and subtle or hidden meanings. I became convinced that I had somehow been accepted into a position in the Philosophy Faculty at Oxford, so much so that one day I even packed up all of my belongings and attempted to order a van to take me to Oxford, where I believed I would be welcomed into the University with open arms and shown to a room! As it happened, the van never showed up, and my belongings stayed in their boxes for several months.

I also composed fantastical letters to fantastical people. I derived great amusement from playing around with language in these letters, and there was a kind of comfort in writing and posting them. At this time I had little regard for the postal service, on whom I was placing a great burden, though occasionally apologetic feelings did surface.

I am sorry to say that there is also a much darker, and much less enjoyable aspect to psychosis, which is depression. In the run up to both of my 'episodes' I experienced long periods of isolation and depression, and my mood has been verging on suicidal on a number of occasions.

I remember one time when I had been lying in bed, literally for weeks, simply experiencing different shades of depression. I was taking a drug called diazepam and was off work, and it was a time when my depression was such that if I ventured out to the park for half an hour in a day that was a great achievement. Sometimes I would lie there for hours, literally believing I was dying. I felt that my body was riddled with disease, and I would focus intently on my breathing, believing at times that I was about to draw my last breaths.

In a state of confusion one time I remember taking an overdose of some medication that I had been prescribed. I knocked back about eight tablets, but I didn't have the intention of ending my life, or even of experimenting with the drug – instead it was an indescribable confusion that led to this action.

During this same psychotic episode I became convinced that I had cancer, and then obsessed that my sister had cancer. I remember being on the bus from Oxford to London with my sister and asking her to squeeze my hand. She must have wondered what I was doing, but really I was testing her strength to get an indication of how deeply she was riddled with the disease. As it turned out, she was fine!

Another time, I became convinced that my father had actually died! How I would know this telepathically it is difficult to say, but I had internally the experience of my father dying. It was like something left my heart, and I burst into tears, and even broke the bad news to my sister who was with me. Needless to say I was rather surprised when I spoke with my father later on and found out he was also perfectly fine.

During this period I also experienced confused identity. I remember going through a lengthy psychiatric assessment, but every word the psychiatrist spoke about me I believed he was speaking about my sister.

Double meanings are another element of the psychosis I experienced. Certain things symbolised other things that they wouldn't normally. I remember in one psychiatric hospital seeing a picture of a bowl of lemons, and I was convinced that I was being mocked somehow – that the patients were somehow being called a bunch of lemons through this picture! I recall that at times I could be having a conversation with someone, and his or her understanding of what we were saying would have been completely different to mine, though we were still able to communicate in a conversational way.

On one occasion my housemate had developed a cough. Each time he coughed it would symbolise some other meaning to me. For instance, a certain cough could mean 'Hello, Steve!' and another cough might mean 'Be quiet'. I was having a conversation with him through his coughs and the responses in my head, but he wouldn't have been aware of what I was experiencing at all. I developed a kind of 'coughing vocabulary', and when I was out and interacting with people in shops for instance, the way they coughed would signify things like their social status and how much space they needed. Truly bizarre!

There was also a deeply spiritual aspect to my psychotic experiences that is very personal to me, and very difficult to convey in a meaningful way.

During my first episode, I had an argument with one of my housemates before leaving the flat barefoot and running around my local borough for several hours. I believed that I was being chased by the police, even though this was not the case. I eventually settled to a walking pace, and with torn and bleeding feet made my way to an adjacent town where I ended up at a mosque. The gentlemen at the mosque gave me clothes, and I proceeded to sleep rough for three nights, living off fruit (I had my wallet with me but only a few pounds), and off donations from the Muslim worshippers. I remember having a conversation with one of the mosque's spiritual leaders, and I even attended a worship service. I believed myself, in a strange way, to be being held hostage by these men as an exchange for the prisoners that were at that time being held captive in Guantanamo Bay! This was obviously a complete fabrication and I was actually treated very well by the men at the mosque.

One of these nights, when I was sleeping rough, I had a particular experience of being drunk without having consumed any alcohol. I was walking along and found an empty whisky bottle on the floor. I picked it up, and as I walked I started to feel drunk, staggering along in an inebriated fashion, but without having drunk a single drop of alcohol. It wasn't that I was *pretending* to be drunk, but rather that I actually experienced drunkenness without alcohol. What

I learned from this experience is that the shift in our mental state that we experience when drunk is *not from the liquid* but rather from God working in our body, mind, and spirit. I now believe that God could bring on a state of drunkenness in any person at any time, if He so chose.

After three days of sleeping rough and mingling with the Islamic community in the town, I found myself walking into a church, which was just yards from the mosque. In a way that I cannot describe, it felt like coming home. A kind lady, a church warden, took me by the hand, and led me at first to the house of the vicar next door (who wasn't in), and then into the main church building. I was offered a cup of tea, and given a truly warm reception. I proceeded to sit down on a pew, and began to pray. God began to speak to me, in a very real way. In the half an hour or so that followed I had the most profound experience of the presence of God, and became aware of the fact that through all I was experiencing and had experienced, God was demonstrating to me His reality and His greatness.

I felt at the time that I was caught up in some kind of a great spiritual battle between Islam and Christianity. And I believe that by leading me at first to a mosque and then to a church, God was trying to teach me something about the relationship between these religions, and that there is only one God, who is in control of all things.

There was an organist playing, rehearsing perhaps, as I prayed in the church that day, and the thought occurred to me that it might be my destiny to become a professional organist. I became acutely aware of how the organ music, the shape and size of the building, the uncomfortable pews – all of this was paying tribute to the greatness of God!

Not long after this a couple of police officers arrived,

and I was given a telephone so that I could make a call to my father. He had been worried about me, and the police wanted to assure him that I was in safe hands. I was taken in a police van to a nearby hospital, where I was assessed by two mental health professionals, and then sectioned under the Mental Health Act. I was then transported to a nearby psychiatric hospital. I appealed against the section and won the appeal, and was discharged from hospital a few weeks later, having been prescribed anti-psychotic drugs.

I am not going to go into great detail here about my experience of being in psychiatric hospital. But suffice to say, it is a very challenging environment, where the whole range of human emotions can be experienced. I have the greatest respect for any person who has been in psychiatric hospital, especially those who are sectioned and kept in hospital for up to six months at a time.

There is a common characteristic of the two times that I experienced psychosis and ended up in hospital. On both occasions, I turned to the Bible for help. I cannot easily convey the significance of this to you, but I can tell you this – that the Bible is a book of profound importance.

I only survived my second spell in hospital because of the Bible, and passages about hope and about God's love. God uses the Bible to talk to people – it is as simple and as complicated as that. During my second spell in hospital, I would pray constantly throughout the day, and I even wrote out the books of Genesis and Matthew. I wrote out important scriptures and stuck them to the wall in the shape of a cross, and cut out the letters Jesus Christ and stuck them above the cross. I went from being a me-centred person to a God-centred person, establishing a real relationship with God through His grace working in my life.

Since leaving hospital that second time, my life has been completely transformed. I am healthy, and happy, and have made a wonderful group of friends through attending a lively and thriving church in central London. Strained family relationships have been restored and I feel that my life has direction and purpose. I am currently studying a postgraduate course in Philosophy and Religion in London, and have a variety of interesting and exciting projects on the go.

Over the last few years, my life's journey has been a challenging, but I dare say not an unusual one. Unique of course, but I suppose every reader will have their own tales to tell; tales of seeking and tales of personal struggles. I have, through all of the experiences recounted in this book, been on a search. The only time I have ever felt that search make sense, is in the light of my new found understanding of what Jesus Christ did for me a little over two thousand years ago, when He died on a cross in great agony so as to allow me and millions of others around the world a new life of hope and abundance.

In the past, I have been a moral and spiritual mess. Now, I feel well, and want nothing more than to live a good, honest, loving, and peaceful life, and to bring praise and glory to the Creator, who has so graciously revealed Himself to me, through a journey of many twists and turns.

Only God can turn a life around. Trust in Him, and never give up hope.

Part Two

My Philosophy

1

Introduction

Philosophy is simple, and don't let anyone tell you otherwise.

Simple in what sense? In the sense that, because you are just as much a philosopher as I am, anything goes. That is to say, in the pursuit of truth, of knowledge, of the meaning of life, and other such philosophical matters, we are in the business of opinion. And everyone's opinion is valid.

Please bear in mind that all that is contained within the pages of this book is not factual. And I mean that in the sense that I do not believe in facts. Even in the domain of science, where so-called facts dictate a way of thinking, I am dubious as to the certainty of assertions that are made. How can anything be definite, factual, in a world that is constantly changing, and where no two moments are ever the same?

This short text aims to capture thoughts that I have had relating to existence, and attempts to portray the way in which I understand the world. I cannot predict the thoughts that you will have when reading these words, but I believe there is a way in which words do communicate ideas, albeit through the activities of God working in the mind and body of a reader at a given moment in time. Therefore I am confident that some or all of this text will provoke some kind of a reaction in you, and I hope that is the case.

As I present my arguments, I will try to use language that is simple and accessible. This is because I believe that every idea that amounts to anything can be communicated in a clear and simple way. If there is anything that I write that you do not understand, please don't take the blame for that, I am as guilty as you are.

In many subjects that are studied today, in schools and universities and so forth, there is a certain style of learning – a certain way of doing things. When working towards an examination in Philosophy, for instance, we are normally asked to study 'key thinkers' who have 'formulated ideas'. The terminology used in study is often complex and burdensome.

This approach has the unfortunate consequence of creating a kind of elitism within the subject. What I mean by that is that only a handful of individuals, relatively speaking, are deemed to be 'intelligent' enough to be accomplished in the subject of Philosophy.

For me, this is a very upsetting state of affairs. I would hate the idea that you would consider yourself to be any less of a philosopher than Aristotle or Plato, than Kant or Descartes, or any of the other philosophers studied in institutions throughout the world. The chances are that if you haven't heard of one or more of those names just mentioned you will feel alienated, and that is precisely the problem, and precisely the state of affairs I wish to help correct.

What alternative way of learning is there, you might ask? Well, my view, quite simply, is that philosophy should focus on ideas rather than thinkers. Philosophy is about a fascination with existence that we all share, and therefore egoism and elitism within the subject really is shameful. Any two people can quite feasibly come up with the same ideas independently of each other, and in the pursuit of wisdom that is philosophy, no one has a right to claim ownership of an idea.

In the following exposition I aim to tackle what are, to me, some of the key questions of philosophy. It will not be a long and tortuous process, but rather, I will aim to capture only the key points I have to make around each particular subject. I will try to progress my arguments in a logical way, though philosophical discussion is no science, and I am not perfect, so please bear these things in mind while you are reading.

Above all, I hope you will enjoy reading this work. In fact, work is a rather dull term for what might be better described as play. Philosophy is a subject that excites me greatly, and I believe there is no better use for anyone's time than to explore the fundamental questions surrounding our existence. So, without further ado, let's commence our exploration by investigating the nature of the human self.

2

Who am I?

First, it is true to say that I exist. What makes me certain of this is that I have an awareness, a consciousness. This consciousness is something that is difficult to define, as it doesn't appear to have attributes. At a push, I might call it awakeness or aliveness. It is stable and unchanging, though the *contents* of the consciousness (including all of the colourful objects I see around me) is changing. The tree sways in the wind. The cars speed past my window. The second hand of the clock ticks.

But am I consciousness itself, the contents of consciousness, or only a part of the contents of consciousness? Do I exist as an entity that is separate from other things, and if so, what is the nature of that entity?

I have a name. Other things have different names. Therefore there must be some distinction, some separateness between other things and me that I am aware of and am able to understand.

Am I perhaps this body that I see when I look down? One thing that helps me to explore this question is my experience of pain. When I pick up a pole and hit the table I feel nothing, and yet when I hit my leg, or my arm, I feel pain. There seems, therefore, to be a difference between my body and other objects. My body is a pain-sensing object, whereas the table isn't.

But does that necessarily mean that the table is any less 'me' than the body that experiences pain? It is true to say that I am experiencing the table and experiencing my body. Visually, they are different shapes, but they are similar in terms of being out there in my awareness. Perhaps, rather than saying "I am a body", it would be more correct to say that "I have a body and a table that are part of the same experience."

Do I really have any reason to believe that objects other than the body are any less 'me' than the body? These other objects come and go as life goes on, but then so does my body, when I am asleep, or when I close my eyes, for instance. What 'I' am must therefore be something that remains while all objects, including my body, come and go.

In order to further illuminate our discussion we can look at the idea of death. What is it that dies when 'I' die? Because I have no experience of my own death it is difficult to say. Death is, in part, the transformation of the body into a different state (we can observe the body of a dead person becoming cold and still and then decaying and rotting.) But what happens to the 'aliveness' or 'consciousness' that I now experience, when I die? This is a mystery. If it endures, we may envisage eternal life. If it doesn't endure, we might envisage eternal nothingness.

Just because I can't remember being a one-year-old doesn't mean that I wasn't once a one-year-old. And in the same way, it is easy to imagine that I might have existed long before birth and simply not have a recollection of that time. Is it possible that this consciousness that I now experience (in which all things are happening), has existed forever?

3

States of Consciousness

I believe that by examining the different states of consciousness human beings experience, we can come to understand something about the nature of reality, and about how God is working in all things always.

I don't always like to make divisions. I see the world as a single universal process animated in the present moment by a living God. However, it is useful for the purposes of discussion to distinguish between three states of mind that commonly repeat on a regular basis. They are the waking state, the dream state, and the dreamless sleep state. I will deal with different states of mind experienced in the waking state in the following chapter.

The waking state is unique in that I identify myself with a body and appear to be moving around in the world. The apparent steady progression of time is an attribute of this waking world, as are my friendships, family relationships, and occupations. I appear to sustain and nourish a body that I experience in this state.

Dreams are rather like intense visualisations that are unaccompanied by the sensory experience of the waking world. In my experience dreams can be extraordinary – even featuring other worlds and unknown people – yet even in their strangeness they feel just as 'real' as the 'real world'.

The dreamless sleep state is one that I presume exists, as

to the best of my knowledge I do not dream constantly all night every night. REM (rapid eye movement) seems to be an indication of dreams (that's when your eyes flutter when you are asleep), and if you observe a friend or partner you will notice that REM doesn't happen all night long (although this doesn't discount the fact that REM might only happen with particular dreams.)

So how do these three states compare, and what can they tell us about the nature of reality?

In the waking state I experience thoughts. In the dream state I experience dreams. It is inconsistent to say that a dream happens to me (passive) but I think a thought (active), because they are similar in terms of both being expressions of the mind impacting on my consciousness. So, either I must be 'doing' both dreaming and thinking, i.e. be in control of them, or they are both 'happening to me'. I cannot be 'doing' them as they are unpredictable and I am unaware of how they happen, therefore they must be 'happening to me'. If they are 'happening to me' then there is no free will in the process. Therefore, God, I would argue, is 'doing' both my thinking and my dreaming. I will have more to say on this in the chapter entitled Free Will.

There is a great deal of interest in lucid dreaming at present. Lucid dreaming is when you feel that you are awake and in control during your dreams. But I wonder, is it any more amazing that I can experience a feeling of free agency in the dream state, than in waking life? The experiences may be wildly different, but the principle is the same. The fact is that you are not in control, even in your lucid dreams. If you were, you might quite happily remain in a blissful state all night every night – you might choose never to awaken!

When we move from being awake to sleeping, from

sleeping to dreaming, and back to waking consciousness again, we are unaware of how we move between these states. It is almost as if we are being brought in and out of sleeping states by some kind of power. What is this power? For all our scientific enquiry, sleeping and dreaming remain quite mysterious. They are mysterious in the same way that the universe as a whole is mysterious, and they are miraculous in the way that the whole of existence is miraculous.

For me, these mysteries will never be explained in terms of neurological processes because there is always the further question of why – why does anything happen at all? The answer, clearly, is that something is doing everything, those things we can explain and those we can't. And that something, I would argue, is God.

4

States of Mind

States of mind differ from states of consciousness in that they are different modes of experiencing in the waking state. One might differentiate between drug-induced states, psychoses, and what might be called a 'normal' state of mind.

How does one differentiate between a psychotic state of mind and a normal state of mind? I believe that we can answer this question in terms of extremes of experience.

Let us first examine what a normal state of mind is. In the normal waking state, one will experience the broad range of emotions (happiness, sadness, anger, frustration, etc) as well as a range of drives (hunger, sexual drives, etc). One might also fantasise, to a certain extent. A degree of sexual fantasy is considered normal by many people, and one might also fantasise about work, or about a sport one is about to play, for instance. When we are children it is quite normal to have fantasies, even very surreal ones.

In adult life we experience ambitions and predictions, and there is a way in which these are also fantasies of the mind. One might go so far as to say that whenever one is using one's imagination, whenever one is in abstract thought, one is fantasising. Even if it is as simple as envisioning what one's dinner will be like, or imagining a scenario portrayed in a book one is reading. The point to note here is that these kinds of fantasies are considered to be normal.

In the psychotic state of mind, fantasies also exist, but they take a more extreme form. A sexual fantasy, for instance, may become an obsession. One might create a fantastical persona for oneself, or for others. One might envisage being involved in complex scenarios that don't exist to others.

The full range of emotions are also experienced during psychosis, but they can become more extreme. One's anger may turn to aggression. One's happiness may become hysterical. Depression may become very serious and perhaps manic.

One might compare certain drug-induced states to psychoses. For instance, after taking hallucinogenic drugs like magic mushrooms, hysterical laughter can be experienced, and this could be described as a form of psychosis. One can experience extreme fear, which can also be present in psychosis. Thought processes can become highly abnormal, and auditory and visual hallucinations experienced, which is also the case with psychosis.

The important point to make here is that there is a similarity between all of these states of mind, and that they differ mainly in the extremeness in which they manifest. If you like, they are varying extremes of the same mental processes.

In the case of psychosis, one might say the individual becomes 'out of control'. But it is interesting to ask the question of what is controlling the mind when I am 'in control'. One might argue that 'I' control the mind in its normal state, and that the drugs are controlling the mind in the drug-induced states. But then the question remains, who or what is controlling the mind in the psychotic state, which is so similar to the drug-induced state? Can one really differentiate between controlling agents in different states of mind?

The answer to me is clear. Our mental processes are under the same control in all of their various states. The controlling power is God.

5

Reality

When examining the fundamental nature of things, it is interesting to look at the difference between the one, and the many. On first impression, it may seem that there are many different things that make up the world. We might say that there are a variety of things that have different characteristics. The spoon is hard, whereas the air is soft; the pen is light, whereas the book is heavy. So it is possible to distinguish between the attributes of different things that make them distinct from one another.

I believe that we come to understand what a thing in itself is through contrast. It is only through a contrast with otherness that anything can be experienced. A spoon only becomes a spoon in relation to what we might call 'not-spoon'. I recognise it visually, for instance, because it contrasts with a background. I recognise its texture, because it is hard as opposed to the softness of the air, for instance. So in this way it is contrast that creates separate things.

Another way of looking at separate things is to view them like snapshots of a part of the total reality. Imagine if you were to hold up an empty picture frame and walk around a park. You might momentarily capture a 'tree' or 'grass', a 'bird' or perhaps a 'pond' within the frame. This might give you the impression of separate objects, but it is interesting to ask, do those things really exist independent of the totality, which we call 'park'? Arguably the park is a single entity, and if we expand this reasoning outward, the universe as a whole is a single entity.

An alternative way of looking at reality is in terms of a single underlying substance.

Some philosophers have argued that there is a single element to which all things can be reduced, whether it be fire, water, or energy. In this view, a single substance changes its form to make objects that embody different characteristics so that when we speak of matter, energy, spoons, or air, we are really talking about the same thing. The physicist might argue that apparently separate things are simply different vibrations of the same particles, or that they are all expressions of the same energy.

When examining the nature of reality we can look at substances, and we can also look at consciousness. Is consciousness itself also part of a single substance that underlies our reality, or is consciousness unique in being distinct from the rest of reality? If I were to say I am conscious of reality, is that making distinctions (between myself, consciousness, and reality) that don't really exist?

Perhaps consciousness could be regarded as the fundamental constituent of reality, even prior to energy, or perhaps energy itself is a kind of consciousness. Perhaps all things are consciousness, manifesting itself in different forms.

Needless to say, there is great debate regarding how anything has come to be in existence at all. If you are a scientist, you might address this problem in terms of a succession of events that began and developed the universe, and that have led to the state of affairs we experience as the present moment. But the problem with causal chains is that they are purely conceptual, and they separate out what is essentially a continuous process into events. In reality, because events flow into one another, there are no separate events.

It is only when we come to understand reality as a single eternal moment that things begin to make sense. You might ask yourself, where is the past now? Where is the future now? They exist in thought form only, and thoughts come and go. One might argue that what comes and goes is not real.

So what is real? What really exists? Only what is stable and unchanging and endures forever can really be classed as real, as everything else can potentially disappear.

I would argue that there are two things that exist forever, and that those two things are intimately interlinked. God, on the one hand, is the creator and sustainer of all things. God is alive now, has always existed and always will. God is invisible, but has the characteristics of omnipotence (all-powerfulness), omniscience (all-knowingness), and omnipresence (God is everywhere), and is the being that animates life and creates change in the cosmos.

On the other hand, there is 'I', which is my experience of awareness or consciousness. It is the experience of life that is ever-present, and it exists regardless of thought and whether I am experiencing a body or not. I can only presume this has always existed, as to imagine anything without the feeling of my aliveness is impossible.

The whole of existence can be seen as a play in which God expresses Himself through an infinite number of things that each experience a sense of separateness. I would hazard a guess that it is only in death that the underlying unity becomes clear, when the apparent separateness of all things (including 'I' and God) will be reunited into their purest, most cohesive form.

6

Infinity

Anyone who has ever grappled with the problem of infinity will acknowledge that it produces in the mind a certain kind of confusion that is like no other. It is a wonderful concept that is deeply mystifying. But why does the infinite throw the mind into such frustrating disarray?

In order to answer this question, we must examine the concept a little more closely.

What we see with infinity is a progression that goes on forever. Some examples of this are infinite time, infinite numbers and infinite causes.

Let us start with time. Time makes divisions of moments, minutes, hours, and so on. But when we ask the question – what exactly is it that time divides into units? – we realise that there is nothing to be found! There is only what we might call a single, boundless moment that has no intrinsic divisions, no beginnings or ends. This is the reality of the situation. So we can say that time exists as a concept, but not in reality.

Can the same be said of numbers? Well, when we speak of one or two or three we are really envisaging degrees of separateness, or put another way, a whole divided up. After all, if you were asked to express the concept of 'three', what else would you do than produce three objects? But in reality, there are no separate objects! There is no way of proving where one object begins and another ends, because all objects are interlinked. The seed, for instance, doesn't exist independently of the soil, the water, the air, the sun, and everything else that helps it to grow.

And what of infinite causes? Cause and effect chains are highly problematic. After all, what is the beginning and end of a specific cause? Take the example of me kicking a football. What caused the football to be kicked? Was it my foot striking the ball, my run up to the ball, my arrival at the football pitch, my birth into existence, or the Big Bang? It is impossible to say. The confusion comes from the very differentiation of the eternal process into separate events, which have no reality, because they are all interlinked.

In conclusion, then, we can clearly see that the problem of infinity is linked to our tendency to divide reality into separate things. What solves the problem of infinity is the remembrance or realisation that are no separate things. There is one eternal moment, and in reality, you can't divide up what is eternal (outside of time) into chunks.

7

God

I have mentioned God several times and it is helpful to examine who or what God is in a little more detail. Conceptual language will never be able to grasp the fullness of God, but one can perhaps use words to point in the direction of who God is. For instance, one might say God is pure creativity, the greatest thing there is, and the animator of all, along with the more commonly mentioned attributes of omnipotence, omniscience, and omnipresence. All of these attributes combined maybe help us to capture something of the essence of what or who God is.

In much of the philosophy I have read, there is a suggestion that it is best to speak of God using poetic rather than descriptive language. I think there is a lot to be said for this idea. I might say, for instance, that God is my fortress. This would not mean, quite obviously, a physical fortress, but the word fortress speaks volumes about God because of the connotations that relate to my understanding of a fortress in the physical world – God is mighty and strong, for instance.

To attempt to write anything about the indescribable awesomeness that is our God is always going to be a treacherous task. This short chapter, therefore, has aimed only to point to a few of God's attributes, and I hope it will help those who have not had a revelation of the reality of God to grasp something of what I mean when I refer to our almighty Creator throughout this work.

8

Time

In the modern world we are obsessed with an idea that the past leads to the future. This is a complete myth – perhaps the biggest of our age. It is a presumption on which so much science is based, and it pervades our culture as well.

Have you ever wondered why there are 60 minutes in an hour but 24 hours in a day? Seconds, minutes, hours, days, months, years – all of these are artificial creations, they have no reality. A simple experiment will help demonstrate this. Start by discarding all the clocks, watches, or other time measuring instruments you have in the room. Then quite simply, try to time a minute. Clap your hands to start, and clap again to stop.

OK, so experiment over, how successful were you? The first thing to realise is that you will never know! It is significant that you will never know because what that tells us is that time is not inside you. You have no way of knowing what a second or a minute or an hour or a month is, independently of some measuring device.

The conclusion we can draw from this is that time is encapsulated in measuring devices, rather than in reality. This might sound obvious to some people, but will be a shocking assertion to others. For if there is no time, how can we talk meaningfully about things as having beginnings?

I would ask you to consider this. What is the beginning of

the elephant? Is it the baby elephant? Is it the foetal elephant? Is it the sperm of the elephant's father, and the egg of its mother, perhaps? Or is it the elephant's father and mother? Or the grandparents of the elephant? We can go back in 'time' forever trying to establish what first caused the elephant, but we won't get anywhere because what we are doing is fabricating! We are creating ideas about a past that does not now exist. It is a futile task. There is an adult elephant that is manifesting now and that is all that we can meaningfully say without conjecture.

I realise that this way of looking at the world has broad-reaching implications. It has implications for science, in terms of how useful attempts are to discover how the universe began, for instance. It has implications for talking therapies like psychotherapy and psychoanalysis, which attempt to look at the present in terms of the past, and see one's present as the result of childhood experiences, for instance.

But maybe we need to shift our focus in the Western World. Maybe we have become so enamoured by time that we have become dependent on it, forgetting all the while its limitations as being a mechanics rather than a reality. It is liberating to remember that we exist outside of time, as bondage to the past and to the future creates a kind of structure in our lives that can inhibit our experience of the present moment, which contains the fullness of God and is all there really is.

9

Events

We talk about things, and we also talk about events. The reality is that no two 'events' are ever exactly the same. Also, because events flow into each other, it is impossible to say where one ends and another begins. All events are really one event. Contrary to the belief of many scientists, we do not live in a mechanical world where things happen in a succession of events, we live in a world that exists now and now only; a present-moment cosmic unfolding that is alive with the animating power of God.

You only need look at a cause and effect chain to see the absurdity of looking at events in the world as though they are mechanical processes. The whole thing is a big bogus mess! Let me explain. For every cause, one will always need to examine what caused the cause, and what caused that cause, and so we can go back indefinitely until one envisages either an 'infinite regress' (causes causing causes forever and ever) or a 'first cause' such as the much-hyped 'Big Bang' which many scientists allege started the universe. But then, of course, there is the question of what caused the Big Bang. With all due respect to the scientists, one has the feeling that the only big bang in question might be of one's head banging against a brick wall!

Rather than being focused on chains of events, it is possible to take a different approach to understanding how reality evolves. If God is alive and in control of all things, then we can see life as a creative process in which a single universal moment is being evolved in accordance with His divine will. This is evident when we look at the way huge ecosystems and communities operate and interact – there is clearly a harmony in their activity, and this can only be due to a single vast coordinating power operating within them.

There is a place for describing events in this world, as events are a way of talking about reality. But we should never lose sight of the fact that separate events do not really exist. If we don't acknowledge the limitations of event-speak then we are living in a dream world, which is something that science does not purport to be doing.

10

Free Will

Have you ever wondered about the distinction between the things that you are doing, and the things that are simply 'happening'?

Let us look at this distinction in terms of our common experience.

As I write this sentence, I would say certain things are 'just happening'. My heart is beating, blood is flowing through my veins (I presume) and my nails and hair are growing (albeit rather slowly). These are all things that I say are happening to me. On the other hand, I might say that I am typing, I am drinking this cup of tea, I am looking at the clock. Those are things that I am doing.

So what makes us draw this distinction? I believe it amounts to an association of 'I' with the body that I witness, for instance, when I look down. When this body is interacting with something, like picking up a pen, or kicking a football, we class this as an activity that I am doing. Conversely, the things that are 'happening' relate either to the inner workings of the body or to things 'out there' in the world at large.

But need we draw this distinction? If we take away for a moment the idea that I am the body, aren't both processes that I am doing, and those that are happening, similar in their activeness and in the sheer fact that they are going on?

Consider the following questions:

> What is causing me to grow? (internal)
> What is causing the tree to grow? (external)
> What is causing the football to be kicked? (action)

The scientist might answer the above questions in terms of distinct cause and effect processes. But as we have already seen, there are always an infinite number of causes contributing to the action of what we perceive to be one event. What really caused the football to be kicked? Was it the movement of my leg? Was it an impulse in the brain telling my leg to move? Was it my arrival at the football pitch? One could go on to describe an infinite number of causes, but the truth is that it happened quite spontaneously!

The answer to our questions, it would seem clear, is that the same being, the same force, is animating all things simultaneously in this moment. After all, the tree and the football and I exist within the same consciousness. The changing agent, the animating force, is God. Because God is capable of doing an infinite number of things simultaneously, we see that all of the above actions can happen at the same time.

As an interesting aside, our use of language often contains clues to help us understand what is really going on. We say "I acted wrongly", or "you're acting strange", so even in our everyday language we are aware that we are like characters acting in a play. This is the way it really is! Whatever you 'do' is what God is doing through you. He is the cosmic director, intimately involved with your every 'act' of free will.

In saying all of this, I am not denying that a sense of free agency does indeed present itself in our human experience.

There is a sense in which I do operate *as though* I am a free agent, making decisions and going about my business. An attribute of God's power is that He can cause us to believe not only that we are individuals in a separate world, but also that we are the ones doing everything! This is bizarre when you think about it – I can raise my arm or nod my head, but I have absolutely no idea how I do it. God only knows how – because God is doing it.

11

Learning

As you read this text, it is what you bring to your reading that gives it meaning. Lines and markings on a page do not in themselves embody any meaning, but rather it is the mind of the reader that brings life to the words.

But what powers our present-moment activity of understanding? Can you really say you have an understanding of mathematics when you are thinking about eating your dinner? Where is the mathematical understanding then? "In my memory", you might say. But what exactly *is* your memory? Have you actually seen it? What does it look like? What are its attributes? Really think deeply about this. I would question whether there is any such thing.

I believe in a much more present-moment understanding of how we come to understand things. I believe that God is working in this moment, and this moment only (that is all there is), and is bringing a feeling of understanding to us through thoughts and feelings, images and recollections that are stored in His cosmic consciousness, rather than in our brains, as is the case in traditional understanding.

I believe that God's scope for bringing images and thoughts into our minds is infinite – there is no limit to the number of things that you or I could think about in any given moment. This is why it is possible to experience unusual and warped states of mind, as is the case in psychoses and drug-induced states.

Knowledge, I would argue, is not something that we store up in our brains. I don't believe that bits of wisdom sit in bits of grey matter in our brains. That to me is absurd. The brain, rather, is a mysterious conduit that God uses in order to transform His infinite knowledge into our present-moment understanding. Thoughts are impressions upon our consciousness, sculpted by God who is the author of all that we think. When neuroscientists talk about the brain, but leave God out of the equation, they are missing the most important part of the puzzle. The brain will never be understood without an awareness that God produces our minds, as well as our physical bodies.

Are we ever really learning anything new? It is interesting that we talk about 'learning to walk', for instance. This makes it seem as though knowledge is required to understand and perform this activity. But the truth is that I am not conscious of how I walk – it just happens! In the same way that I do not learn to breathe, or to grow my hair; all actions (whether internal or external) are quite spontaneous! Does the apple tree learn how to grow apples?!

Things happen spontaneously because God, who is in control of everything, is doing them.

12

Language and Symbols

When we use language, we are on the whole experiencing a process of tension and resolution. For instance, technical terms that one doesn't understand cause a feeling of tension, while technical terms that one does understand cause a feeling of relief. Complex and long sentences provide a tense feeling, while short, simple sentences produce a more pleasant, enjoyable sensation.

Punctuation also affects our emotional response. A question mark produces a different feeling to an exclamation mark. What we are dealing with when we hear and read language is subtle shifts or impressions in conscious feeling. That is what 'understanding' is – it is a feeling in the body rather than what has often been called a cognitive process.

Examine what happens within you as you read the following sentence:

It was a bright, sunny day, but death was coming for him.

When I read that sentence, a darker, heavier feeling becomes present when the word 'death' is read. This is very subtle, but it is a shift in the way I feel. We must remember that words are just markings on a page that mean nothing in themselves, so the process of understanding must come from somewhere else – from within, you might say. In this way I believe understanding to be an act of God working in us, who brings to our consciousness different impressions as we read.

It is true to say that each sentence we can utter has a different quality, different attributes, and a different character. No two readings of a sentence, even by the same person, will provoke precisely the same response in the body/mind. This is why the process of linguistic analysis is to a large extent useless. To try to apply rules to a medium that is both contextual (language is always used within a context) and where no two sentences are ever read in an identical way, is to embark on a rather futile task. Even when I read the following...

Tonight there will be a full moon. Tonight there will be a full moon.

...there is a very subtle difference in the response in me when reading the first and second sentences, even though formally they are identical!

Let us explore another, mathematical example. We would generally agree that the following makes sense:

$$2 + 2 = 4$$

But why is this so? What gives that expression a feeling of 'rightness'? How can the symbol 2 mean anything? Does 2 mean anything? Isn't 2 also just a mark on the page?

As an experiment, is it possible to break the habitual process and look at the following sum in a way that makes it *feel* correct?

$$2 + 2 = 5$$

Arguably, it is! For instance, if 2 represents the mental image of a cat, and 5 represents the mental image of 2 cats. Or, alternatively, if 2 carries the mental weight of 3 and 5 the mental weight of 6. Admittedly, you may have to think hard about this in order to make it work, but it does seem to be possible.

To end this chapter, there is an interesting question on which you might like to speculate. What do you see below?

@ @

The point is that even with this simple question it is possible to produce an infinite number of answers. One might say there are two things (two @ signs), four things (two 'a's and two circles around them), three things (two @ signs and a white background) or only one thing (the @ signs together), and I could go on!

What is the significance of this argument? Well, it is important to examine whether there is any absolute reality to what is 'out there' in my awareness, or whether understanding is purely an activity of the mind. It would seem that there is something 'out there' (there is a subject under discussion) but that any attempt to grab that something by way of a description is futile. This is because whenever we try to catch hold of something, to define it, we create divisions. However, all divisions are arbitrary – they simply do not exist in reality.

What the above examples demonstrate is that the mental associations we make with symbols are changeable, and therefore symbols in themselves, without the 'translating' quality of the mind, are meaningless. We quite literally bring symbols to life through impressions that arise in our body/ mind as we read. But from where do these impressions arise? And what causes them to arise? Surely they are the activity and entertainment of our omnipotent God.

13

The Meaning of Life

Imagine if you were God, and had all power, all knowledge, and all things at your disposal. You could do absolutely anything, with the only limitation being that nothing could ever be separate from you. What would you do?

You might start off with a pure 100% awareness of your simplest form, God. This would be a you without any of the attributes we associate with objects, and only you. No time, no space. Pure aliveness, pure nothingness, pure God.

You might want to experiment with this aliveness, and begin by creating a few things, simple things. You might cause part of yourself to be bright and call it light, and another part dim and call it darkness. That might satisfy you for some time, but then you may feel a desire to experiment further, and realise that by altering part of yourself you can create different shades of light, or colours. You might create a rainbow of light the size of a universe. How enjoyable and fascinating this would be to do!

And then, after playing around with light and colour for a few millennia, you might want a new challenge. And so you start condensing parts of yourself into a solid form called matter, and create a few different shapes, simple shapes. And then you realise that by holding a distilled part of yourself in a certain way, you can give the appearance of objects. You can create as many as you want, move them around, and even thrust them into each other! You might well marvel at your creation.

And then, as the aeons pass by, you have the most incredible, wonderful idea. You could create complex objects and create within them the impression that they are entities-in-themselves; that like you, they are beings! They could even interact with each other. You could be the grand puppeteer in a huge universe filled with creatures, and you could create the creatures in such a way that they don't even have to know you exist. So overjoyed would you be with this idea that you would create thousands and then millions of these things in different forms, and give them all names.

You decide to give the people that you create the experience of emotions, in order to reflect the spectrum of reality that exists within your own experience. Like you, your creations will experience wholeness and bliss, but also loneliness and isolation. You hold within your nature both the bliss of absolute consciousness, and the pain of being eternally alone, and you decide that your creations will experience both aspects of your predicament in order to get a taste of the yin and yang of existence.

But still, your potential for elaboration on these marvellous creations is unfulfilled, and you wonder what you should do next. How about a story, you say. Everyone knows that a story needs a beginning, a middle, and an end, and so you invent time and memory, to give the impression that things are moving along. How marvellous all this is, you think to yourself.

And so you come up with a story line that will last for thousands of years, and that comprises a wonderful display of who you are through your creation. You decide that you will use a single being that you have created in order to display your infinite power and ultimately loving nature. So you create a man named Jesus Christ, who embodies so much of what you are, and you call him your Son. You make him famous on Earth, and display your love for him and for other human beings through miracles, through healing, and through compassion. Through your human creations you make a book about this man and his life, where the story can be captured. The book, called The Bible, is perfect in its imperfection, as is the case with all that you so delicately and masterfully create (Oh how you love to give the impression of independence, frailty, and free will!)

You use the story of Jesus Christ as a means of reconciliation, of bringing people who you have caused to feel separate from you back into a knowledge of and relationship with you. You call this salvation, and make it the purpose of human life on Earth.

What human beings will never know is the future that you have in store for them. Through your grace, and your acting in their lives, they might be blessed with faith in you; however it is your intention that they never fully know or understand your purposes in this life. The whole of life is lived under the shadow of a mysterious event called death, and this brings anticipation to the whole thing.

God is exploring Himself through His creation. Each of us is an important and unique part of God's plan, and of the totality. It is God's eternal occupation to 'do' life!

Epilogue

Since completing this book Steven has experienced a third spell in psychiatric hospital, and is currently being treated for Schizoaffective disorder. He remains hopeful and in good spirits, and is eager to make a good recovery, and to continue his academic work and writing.

Steven's thought in relation to Christianity has developed somewhat since this book was written. He is a friend of many Christians, but finds fault with the Christian idea that there has been an estrangement from – a 'fall' – away from God. If God is everywhere and in everything, as the author fervently believes He is, then to talk of separateness from God, and of human beings having free will (which is what Christians generally believe), is wrong. This important theological point is discussed further on Steven's blog, www.perfectchaos.org, so feel free to visit the site and join the discussion.

Steven requests that this book be passed on to others, including those who have experienced mental health problems and who work in mental health, for their interest and understanding. His hope is that this book will be relevant to many people from diverse backgrounds at some point during their journey through life.

Helpful Resources

Contact Steven: riversofchange@gmail.com

Steven's blog: http://www.perfectchaos.org/
Steven's website: http://www.stevencolborne.com/

Mental Health Charities in the UK:

Rethink: http://www.rethink.org/
Mental Health Foundation: http://www.mentalhealth.org.uk/
Mind: http://www.mind.org.uk/
Sane: http://www.sane.org.uk/

Steven advises that if you think you might be experiencing psychosis or other mental health problems you should speak to a doctor as soon as possible. For advice, you can call the Sane Helpline in confidence between 6pm and 11pm on 0845 767 8000.